YOUR KNOWLEDGE HAS VALUE

- We will publish your bachelor's and master's thesis, essays and papers

- Your own eBook and book - sold worldwide in all relevant shops

- Earn money with each sale

Upload your text at www.GRIN.com
and publish for free

Eugen Andri

The Genesis of Modern U.S.-American Drama: Lillian Hellman, "The Children's Hour" (1934)

GRIN Verlag

Bibliografische Information der Deutschen Nationalbibliothek:

Die Deutsche Bibliothek verzeichnet diese Publikation in der Deutschen National-bibliografie; detaillierte bibliografische Daten sind im Internet über http://dnb.d-nb.de/ abrufbar.

Dieses Werk sowie alle darin enthaltenen einzelnen Beiträge und Abbildungen sind urheberrechtlich geschützt. Jede Verwertung, die nicht ausdrücklich vom Urheberrechtsschutz zugelassen ist, bedarf der vorherigen Zustimmung des Verlages. Das gilt insbesondere für Vervielfältigungen, Bearbeitungen, Übersetzungen, Mikroverfilmungen, Auswertungen durch Datenbanken und für die Einspeicherung und Verarbeitung in elektronische Systeme. Alle Rechte, auch die des auszugsweisen Nachdrucks, der fotomechanischen Wiedergabe (einschließlich Mikrokopie) sowie der Auswertung durch Datenbanken oder ähnliche Einrichtungen, vorbehalten.

Imprint:

Copyright © 2012 GRIN Verlag GmbH
Druck und Bindung: Books on Demand GmbH, Norderstedt Germany
ISBN: 978-3-656-28503-8

This book at GRIN:

http://www.grin.com/en/e-book/201473/the-genesis-of-modern-u-s-american-drama-lillian-hellman-the-children-s

GRIN - Your knowledge has value

Der GRIN Verlag publiziert seit 1998 wissenschaftliche Arbeiten von Studenten, Hochschullehrern und anderen Akademikern als eBook und gedrucktes Buch. Die Verlagswebsite www.grin.com ist die ideale Plattform zur Veröffentlichung von Hausarbeiten, Abschlussarbeiten, wissenschaftlichen Aufsätzen, Dissertationen und Fachbüchern.

Visit us on the internet:

http://www.grin.com/

http://www.facebook.com/grincom

http://www.twitter.com/grin_com

Contents

1. Introduction………………………………………………………………………….3
2. The Role of Women in Society in the 20th Century and Historical Context…...4
3. The Contribution of Women Writers in the Development of Modern American Drama. Lillian Hellman……………………………………………………………...5
4. The Children´s Hour………………………………………………………………..8
5. Sexuality in The Children's Hour…………………………………………………..9
6. Gender in *The Children´s Hour*. Good and Evil?..11
   - 6.1. Young Mary Tilford…………………………………………………….12
   - 6.2. Mr. Amelia Tilford……………………………………………………….13
   - 6.3. Karen Wright and Martha Dobie………………………………………13
7. Conclusion…………………………………………………………………………..15
8. Literary Sources……………………………………………………………………17

1. Introduction

In terms of this essay I am going to explore the genesis of modern American Drama.

This topic is quite extensive in scope, and that's why I want to focus my attention on women authors who wrote about women and about their place in the society of that time.

In the beginning of my essay I will explore the role of women in the society of the USA at the beginning of the previous century. I will examine what made women change.

In the next part of the essay I will examine the contribution of women writers in the literature of the USA at that period of time and specifically the contribution of Lillian Hellman on the basis of her play "The Children´s Hour". I am interested in topics and issues that she takes under consideration in her play, and what actually Lillian Hellman wanted to achieve by writing and staging it.

In the last part of my essay I will examine the gender and sexuality represented in "The Children´ s Hour" by Lillian Hellman and, finally, I will present my thought about the contribution of women writers and especially the contribution of Lillian Hellman to the genesis of the modern American Drama.

2. The Role of Women in Society in the 20th Century and Historical Context

Lillian Hellman wrote *The Children´s Hour* in 1934. It was a time when the United States was experiencing the consequences of the Great Depression and the economy of Europe was also suffering. The nation was too busy fighting against poverty and unemployment. Because of the shortage of men in the First World War, many women were able to find jobs and feel less dependent on men. Women had to work in factories and hospitals to replace the men who had to fight but The Great Depression and unemployment has slowed this process.

The men were in an emotional crisis because they could no longer earn enough money. Some men had no work at all. Some men did not feel like a man in the fullest sense of the word. It was also the time when women struggled for their rights. Women still did not have the same rights as men at that time. Up to 1919-1920's, the main subject of the struggle was the right to vote. The early women's movement was just a struggle for the expansion of the natural rights which men had. In the 19th century a woman's task was to keep the house in order and to please her husband. The responsibilities of the men entailed earning money and controlling the family finances. The man was the master of the family and had the final say on controversial issues. The woman from birth was given fewer rights and no matter at what age she was. A wife, a widow, a sister or a daughter had always been on the sidelines after their husbands, brothers or sons. After having voted for the first time in 1922, women were able to fight for their rights to a greater extent. Women were emboldened to demand more personal freedoms. They began to wear more short skirts, their hair was cut shorter than in the past, smoking and drinking alcohol in public, despite the illegality of consuming alcohol in public. Women began to speak out against such misnomers like "men sexuality". That time men affairs were taken as appropriate and healthy and women affairs like a kind of corruption and evil. (Kimberly M. Radek)

According to Associate Professor Judith E. Barlow[1], the years from 1930 to 1960 were even less propitious for women. "The Great Depression of the 1930s and then the Second World War moved what were considered "women´s issues" to the back burner, while the Cold War period ushered in a reactionary attitude toward gender

---

[1] Barlow, E. Judith Plays by American Women 1930-1960. Applause. New York, London 1994 p.vii

roles as well as politics. (Barlow vii) *The Children's Hour* refers to Depression only by remarking the period of time that Karen and Martha needed to build the school and the cost of a telephone call or a taxi.

3. The Contribution of Women Writers in the Development of Modern American Drama. Lillian Hellman

Bloom argues[2] that the age of American theatre is born of a double movement one artistic and the other political, the former political, the latter conditioned by a general cultural shift. Bloom states [3]that in the first two decades of the century the influence of Strindberg and Ibsen, Yeats and Nietzsche made American theater international. Bloom adds[4] that American theatre became international because of isolation and through isolationism." By the 1940s America was poised to dominate the drama of the English speaking world and the great age of American theater was about to commence." (Bloom: 4)

[...] "born in this century[5], the American Drama has acted both as a reflection and as a commentary of the dominance, power and sometimes corruption of the American democratic dream." (Bloom vii) Eugene O'Neil, Tennessee Williams, Susan Glaspell, Imamu Amiri Baraka and Arthur Miller continue to deal with the issues pertinent to the "American Century" whether these are about gender, color, political oppression or political correctness." (Bloom: vii)

As I have written above the role of women changed and this [...] "brought, disintegration of traditional roles and the consequent stress in family relationships" (Friedman: 72). No wonder that in the literature began to appear works, which were devoted to the theme of women. Barlow argues[6] that in that period male producers and directors dominated and women writers had to face the demise of many little theatres. Certainly the literary works of women existed before. Jordan Miller argues[7]

---

[2] Bloom, Clive. American Drama Macmillian 1995 p.3
[3] Ibid
[4] Ibid
[5] we are talking about 20th century
[6] Barlow, E. Judith Plays by American Women 1930-1960. Applause. New York, London 1994 p.vii
[7] Miller, Y. Jordan and Frazer, L. Winfred. American Drama between the Wars: A Critical History P. 14

that [...If one is to search American Drama for women playwrights of any stature before 1900, the list is sparse to the point of virtual nonexistence. Miller states[8] that until the new century American women dramatics haven't contributed anything worthy of attention. Miller argues[9] that women writers bring their contribution in writing and backstage labors, combined with impact of the alternative little theatres for which they often wrote. "These factors were vitally important in moving the American drama into the artistic world of the 20th century "(Miller: 14). What else is new? According to Bigsby [10]women were literarily seen as the mere observers of history, not its engine. Bigsby argues[11] that their realm was a private one and that of men was a public one. Women were seen only in relation to men. For women writers and feminists of that period of time, there was a possibility to change things and to confront the existing hierarchy of values and concerns. "These concerns constitute feminist themes in that they portray the social and psychological restrictions placed upon women in a male dominant society, as well as the attitudes and values of women who confront these restrictions." (Friedman: 72)   Friedman also states[12] that in that period women's equality had been a powerful social issue and feminist concerns were often central to plays written by women.

"Feminism as theme should not be understood as simply a call for women's rights on the part of the playwright or her characters. Rather, it may be a statement about feminine consciousness, the feelings and perceptions associated with a female character's identity as a woman. As Sydney Kaplan asserts, the feminism of a writer may be reflected in "a consideration of the effect upon women's psyches of the external events around them." (Quoted at Sharon Friedman: 70)

According to Friedman[13] the early women´s movements prompted women writers to pursue a certain freedom of expression and to express themselves in drama. Friedman states that women writers tried to dramatize the social questions of the

---

[8] Miller, Y. Jordan and Frazer, L. Winfred. American Drama between the Wars: A Critical History p. 14
[9] Ibid
[10] Bigsby, C.W. E. Modern American Drama 1945-2000 Cambridge university press 2000 p.317
[11] Ibid
[12] Friedman, Sharon "Feminism as theme in Twentieth-Century American Women´s Drama" American Studies 25.1 (1984):69-89.
[13] Ibid. p.70

day. Barlow argues[14] that in various periods, - the crucial dramas social problems were racism, classism and sexism.

"For women playwrights this often meant exploring the condition of women as a social and psychological phenomenon at the base of a movement for social change" (Friedman: 70)

Friedman argues[15] that even during periods when feminism was not a popular topic for writers, and women's issues were not obvious in drama, the critics may often discern themes that were in effect statements about women's lives, embedded in the major issues of a work and often ignored in interpretation. Friedman states[16] that

[...] "feminist criticism underscores the need to listen to women recreate their own experiences through art, and to discern areas of commonality which grow out of their designation as a group, and which affect creative vision." (Friedman: 70)

Barlow argues[17] that very often critic's attitudes against women were condescending, if not scornful. Barlow cites a critic of that day George Jean Nathan who said [...] "that even the best of our women writers (by which he meant Lillian Hellman) falls immeasurably short of the mark of our best masculine. Male play writer's use "over-intensification and elaboration of emotions" while women dramatics do so because it is unavoidable by nature" Nathan argued that women lack "complete objectivity" because they are too emotional. [...] he concluded that the beauties are wrong" (quoted in Barlow: viii)

According to Griffin and Thorsten, [...] "critics saw Hellman as influenced by Ibsen in her careful plotting, social realism, and use of violence Jacob Adler cites Martha´s suicides, Mary´s extortion of money from Peggy and her blackmail of Rosalie as reminiscent of Ibsen´s technique." (Quoted Griffin and Thorsten p. 35) In the next part of my essay, I will explore the main topics of the play.

---

[14] Barlow, E. Judith Plays by American women 1930-1960. Applause. New York London 1994 p. xxviii
[15] Friedman, Sharon. Feminism as Theme in Twentieth-Century American Women´s Drama. American Studies 25.1, 1984, p.69
[16] Ibid. p.70
[17] Barlow, E. Judith Plays by American Women 1930-1960. Applause. New York, London 1994

4. The Children´s Hour

The Children´s Hour was the first play of Lillian Hellman and ran longer than any other Hellman play. This play was based on a real case which happened in Scotland but Hellman adapted several aspects. "The play´s opening gives us a descent glimpse of normal, everyday goings-on in the girls school, a social organism through Hellman begins her dramatic examination of the values of the society in which we live, the mores taught to the young through our educational system" (Margaret Booker: 61)

Margaret Booker briefly described the play as "A child´s manipulation of a lie containing a social/ sexual taboo wreaks havoc on the school and its teachers and forces the public to question whether the proceedings and mores of society are indeed just" (Margaret Booker: 63)

In my opinion *The Children's Hour* - is a play more about the most severe consequences of rumors (in this case, the rumors about the alleged homosexuality) than about homosexuality itself? „This is not really a play about lesbianism, but about a lie, said Lillian Hellman, describing *The Children´s Hour* to the reporter. (Quoted Griffin and Thorsten p. 27) A commercial and critical success, the play was nonetheless banned in Boston, London, and Chicago, and its failure to win the Pulitzer Prize was widely attributed to its controversial subject matter. The play is one of the first dealing with matters of homosexuality. "Lillian Hellman was attacked for presenting lesbianism as a "painful, defeating experience" which occurred within a heterosexual rather than lesbian community, and this in a play in which such a lesbian experience is in effect problematic." (Bigsby: 325) Some scholars and critics of Lillian Hellman, argue[18] that she was a bisexual in nature and her personality one way or another is present in the play. The laws in that period of time did not allow the presentation in theater and films of homosexual scenes and homosexuality was shown with a "caution, prudence and restraint," which in fact, resounds with the famous saying of Vito Russo[19] (an American LGBT activist, film historian and author)

---

[18] More about : Anderlini-D'Onofrio, S. The Lie with the Ounce of Truth: Lillian Hellman's Bisexual Fantasies
[19] Brenshoff Harry M. and Sean Griffin Queer images: a history of gay and lesbian film in America. — USA: Rowman & Littlefield Publishers, Inc., 2006 .p. 95

"To see homosexuality as a dirty secret," In this way the play the love of Martha for Karen is presented. When Martha finally discovers what she feels for Karen, she describes herself as "incorrect", "guilty" and "patient," which leads to suicide.

I cannot imagine how shocking the play was in 1934, then, if now, when all these topics are discussed freely on every corner, it is still a pretty touchy topic. But in addition to homosexual love theme In my opinion Hellman showed the great strength of a lie, the pressure of society under the laws created by men, as well as doubts about loved ones and one´s self. The play involves rather complex topics of personal, intimate relationships between people (women). Nobody will be surprised now by lesbian relationship. But even now it is not easy to avoid whispering and slightly veiled censure. I am sure that even now such a history may have happened a second time, because society has always been wary of "others." In the next parts of my essay, I will examine briefly how female sexuality and characters are presented in the play *The Children's Hour*.

5. Sexuality in *The Children's Hour*

Mary Titus argues[20] that American theatres in the late 1920s and early 1930s presented several more or less controversial plays exploring the dangerous attraction of lesbianism, particularly to young women in all female environments. Titus adds that between 1926 and 1933, there were a few plays which explored lesbianism (The Captive, Winter Bound and Girls in Uniform) but the best known of such works is Lillian Hellman´s *The Children´s Hour*. Titus states[21] that Hellman´s plays, like the other explorations of lesbianism, [...] both reflects and participates in the cultural revision of women´s sexuality that occurred in the early twentieth century. Titus adds[22] that *The Children´s Hour* emerges as a crucial document, for it not only provides insight into Lillian Hellman´s complex response to contemporary sexual

---

[20] Titus, Mary. Murdering the Lesbian: Lillian Hellman's The Children's Hour Tulsa Studies in Women's Literature.Vol. 10, No. 2 (Autumn, 1991), p. 215
[21] Ibid
[22] Ibid

ideology, it is also illuminates the struggles of her female contemporaries." (Mary Titus: 215)

Serena Anderlini-D'Onofrio argues[23] that the two female protagonists in the play Karen and Martha form a labial duo, a figure of two-in-one at the center of the drama. "In the play's diegetic organization, this figure comes to symbolize the interdependence that characterizes female subjectivity and relationships. The patriarchal order can only understand the two women's emotional and intellectual interdependence as "unnatural" for it bypasses the phallic symbols around which this order is organized. This is what causes the two to be constructed as lovers." (Serena Anderlini-D'Onofrio :10)

The rejection of a homosexual label for the characters of *The Children´s Hour* is according to Serena Anderlini-D'Onofrio[24], an admixture of homophobia and a pre-discursive sense of bisexuality. She adds that […] "for Hellman desire was always multidirectional, and yet, due to the phobias she internalized, it would remain such only in potentiality. Yet in the body of the drama, Hellman emphasizes the moral integrity of the lesbian position, and the dilemmas of a bisexual woman's compromises. "(Serena Anderlini-D'Onofrio: 13) the concept of a separate women´s sphere became, as Titus states[25], […]"potentially threatening and divisive, for it directed women´s sexual and economic power away from the heterosexual establishment." (Titus: 215)

Serena Anderlini-D'Onofrio argues[26] that the play is inflected with the period's antifeminism and homophobia, and Lillian Hellman presented a female character who expresses her love for another woman, and this love is important enough for her to commit suicide. "This is certainly a challenge to the phallocentric canon, wherein the traditional tragic female protagonist kills herself for a man, like Iokaste, Gertrude, Ophelia, Phedra and many others. "(Serena Anderlini-D'Onofrio: 13)

---

[23] Anderlini-D'Onofrio, S. The Lie with the Ounce of Truth: Lillian Hellman's Bisexual Fantasies. University of Puerto Rico at Mayaguez.
[24] Ibid. 9
[25] Titus, Mary. Murdering the Lesbian: Lillian Hellman's The Children's Hour
Tulsa Studies in Women's Literature. Vol. 10, No. 2 (Autumn, 1991), p. 215
[26] Serena Anderlini-D'Onofrio. The Lie with the Ounce of Truth: Lillian Hellman's Bisexual Fantasies. University of Puerto Rico at Mayaguez, p. 13

Suicide is not the end of the play and Hellman continues the story on a positive and straight (heterosexual) note where Miss Tilford convinces Karen to think about getting married to Joe.

6. Gender in *The Children´s Hour.* Good and Evil?

Friedman argues[27] that Hellman does not present what have been termed women's issues as the central focus of any of her plays, in characteristic style, she does emphasize economics. "Her women characters are often portrayed against the socio-economic structures that create and perpetuate their roles. Friedman states[28], that Hellman's characters, though personally and morally responsible for their actions, are almost always portrayed within a social framework, their motives rooted in social forces. Indeed, because Hellman does not stereotype women, but rather portrays them as fully defined individuals shaped by complex political, social and psychological forces, it is not anti-feminist that this playwright has created one of the most destructive women characters in the history of the theatre. Hellman's characterizations of women may appear harsh; she affords her audience the opportunity to explore the conditions of a woman's life which may lead to manipulating, possessive and "emasculating" behavior." (Friedman: 81)

"Critics have often called *The Children´s Hour* a melodrama. Those who have done so, see Karen and Martha as "good" characters who are victimized by "evil" child Mary Tilford. To Barret H. Clark and Brooks Atkinson, Mary Tilford is monster. Even Hellman´s most perceptive critic calls her "the embodiment of pure evil. If the Children´s Hour is the story of a sweet little teacher done to death by----a "tyrannical child" then we must concur with Barret Clark´s reading in of the play´s ultimate meaning: "--- here is evil----make the best of it". (Quoted Philip M. Armato p.1)

---

[27] Friedman, Sharon. Feminism as Theme in Twentieth-Century American Women´s Drama. American Studies 25.1, 1984
[28] Ibid. p.80-81

Armato states [29]that Lillian Hellman defended her play against critics who labeled it a melodrama. Hellman held the opinion that as an author she had no right to see characters as good or evil. She said a journalist reminded her of her own words which claimed that *The Children´s Hour* was about goodness and badness. Lillian Hellman replied that goodness and badness is different from good and evil. She also added that her intent was not to describe the conflict between two good teachers and an "evil" child when she wrote the play. In the next part of my essay I am going to clarify the substance of the play and to examine the women characters labeled as "good" and "evil". (Quoted Philip M. Armato p.1)

6.1. Young Mary Tilford

Children often lie and sometimes much more cruelly than adults. Probably, at their age, there is still no clear understanding of the consequences. They do not understand the scale of the disaster. The protagonist Mary Tilford is a good example. In my opinion she is a very unpleasant character. Mary is extremely hysterical, lying recklessly, artfully blackmails and endlessly trying to blame all in her misadventures, while drawing attention to herself. It is easy for her to slander her teachers, accusing them of having an affair and to manipulate her classmates. I have to admit that she is good in lying and she knows how to lie convincingly. "The fact that Mary´s lie is of a sexual nature intensifies its impact in the thirties, children, especially girls, were shielded from sexual information and were believed to be uninterested in sex until late puberty. That is why Mary´s lie succeeds so effectively. Adults in her community find it inconceivable that she should know about a lesbian relationship unless she had seen actual evidence of it. Mary is clever enough to disguise how much she has learned from reading illicit French novels." (Griffin and Thorsten p. 30-31). Thus, describing what she allegedly" saw", she easily persuaded her grandmother. She ruins the lives of her teachers, despite the fact, that it was only a child´s lie, which could be easily discovered without the "help" of her grandmother and credulous public opinion. If so it could have ended very differently. In contrast to the "highly

---

[29] Armato, Philip M. "Good and Evil" in Lillian Hellman´s The Children´s Hour. Educational Theatre Journal Vol. 25, No. 4 (Dec., 1973), p.p. 443-447. Published by: The Johns Hopkins University Press

moral society", Karen and Martha quickly realized what the goal of the girl was, but the counter-measures taken were insufficient.

Thus, I can sum up, that Mary is not "evil" in the play. She is definitely ill-mannered, but still a child and the terrible consequences of her lies become real only because of the society which her grandmother embodies.

6.2. Mr. Amelia Tilford

According to Griffin and Thorsten" Mrs. Amelia Tilford is a type who appears in mostly of all Hellman´s plays. She is described as "[…] a wealthy widow who has been content to be provided for handsomely first by her father and then by her husband. Mrs. Tilford is a kind of woman who does not think for herself but has inherited her views, principles, and status from the men in her life. Because her principles are hers only superficially, Mrs. Tilford deserts them when she is confronted with a crisis." (Griffin and Thorsten p. 30)

I think that Mrs. Tilford is a kind of good woman but also self-righteous and very stubborn. Until the last minute she was sure she was right, and had no idea that Mary has used her. In my opinion, she is also a victim of its. She was convinced that Mary was an innocent child in such matters as lesbianism..... Because of Mary´s lie, Miss Tilford was "forced" to act and caused the suicide of Martha and as a result a complete emotional devastation of Karen and probably desolation of her own. She knows that full restitution is impossible.

I can sum up that Mrs. Tilford as an image of the decent society is a central character of the play and she is not "evil". I think that not a suicide is crucial to the final scene but the issues, which develop as a result of suicide.

6.3. Karen Wright and Martha Dobie

Karen Wright is a friend of Martha and a partner in a school. She is young (29) and attractive. Her students respect her. She is a good teacher and has the same respect from all her students, including Mary. Mary does not have any preferences, despite the fact that her grandmother is the patron of the school. She can also be described as an emotionally stable person. She is the kind of woman who earns her own money and therefore the independence and power that money could give her. She doesn't need men (a husband) in her business. Martha Dobie is also a young woman and a partner of Karen. She is described as nervous and high-strung. She is not as self-assured as Karen. She is not able to deal with her hidden identity and takes her own life. Both women command attention during the whole play. "They are competent, intelligent and committed to their work but differ in the degree to which they are independent." (Griffin and Thorsten p. 30-31) Griffin and Thorsten state that Karen is more determined and self-sufficient, and Karen can act more firmly. It is Karen's small capital they used to found a school. So, they are both not on an equal footing. It was also Karen who has enough courage to broach the subject of lesbianism, saying "But this isn't a new sin they tell us we've done. Other people aren't destroyed by it." Griffin and Thorsten believe[30] that Karen speaks as one of whom the charge is external, imposed on them by the outside world. Martha, on other hand, internalizes that charge and sees herself through the lens society holds to her. She is convicted that it was always something "wrong" with her and Mary's lie seems to offer a plausible explanation of the truth about herself. "Martha convicts herself of a thought crime and summarily executes herself" "Martha may be mistaken about herself, for one of the awful powers of such a lie is to convince its victims to believe the image of themselves devised by their oppressors." (Griffin and Thorsten 35)

At the end of the play, Karen does not return to Joe, as that would require a happy ending. After the funeral of Martha, Karen goes alone. The play does not answer what her real orientation is - homosexual, heterosexual or bisexual, suggesting that it does not matter. What really matters is that Karen is shown a woman who has the

---

[30] Griffin, Alice and Thorsten, Geraldine. Understanding Lillian Hellman. University of South Carolina Press, 1999, p.34

most poise and ability to decide her fate, the one who is capable (unlike Martha) to rebel against the intolerance of that time.

7. Conclusion

In this paper I have examined the genesis of the modern American Drama and the contribution of Lillian Hellman on the basis of her play "The Children´s Hour"

In the first part of my essay I came to the conclusion that the Great Depression in the USA and the First and the Second World Wars brought significant changes to the economic, cultural and social life of America. After women took part in voting, they did not stop their efforts in demanding personal freedom. The literary world has also changed. Women writers, whose contribution to American drama was not significant before, took the opportunity to write and put the pieces first in small theaters, and then go out to a wider audience. Being under the influence of Ibsen and Strindberg, American women writers devoted their works to the theme of women. The changes affected mostly the female characters. If in earlier plays, the female characters were portrayed only as a supplement to the male images, now they were coming to the fore and raising such topics as the condition of women as a social and psychological phenomenon. The crucial topics were also the women´s equality and such social problems such as sexism, classism and racism.

Lillian Hellman with her play *The Children´s Hour* gained success in spite of a rather controversial subject matter. The public outcry as a result of the girl's lie turned Karen and Martha into real rogues. In my opinion, lesbianism and good and evil, were not the main ideas of Lillian Hellman. I think Hellman showed the tragic love of a female character who was in love with other woman. Sooner or later, having understood the truth, Martha would realize her terrible choice between eternal solitude and death. I think Martha is the main hero of the play. It is Martha´s tragedy to stay close to a loved one seeing her just as a friend. The tragedy made worse by the fact that it is not heterosexual love, as a relationship between a man and a woman quite often turns into love affair. Martha has no chance of reciprocal feelings and Karen has a fiancé. From the emotional point of view the scene of a declaration of love is very deep and touching. Not being understood by society, Martha committed suicide. At the end of the play Karen leaves the city not broken and ready to decide her fate. I can describe the final scene with the aphorism "What doesn't kill us, makes us stronger".

Thus, in my opinion, the characters of Martha and Karen in *The Children's Hour* was the contribution of Lillian Hellman to the modern American Drama. Hellman has shown the sexual and economic power of a woman character apart from the heterosexual society. That was a significant change in exploring the condition of women as a social and psychological phenomenon and rebelled against the literary traditions where the female character kills herself for a man.

9. Literary sources:

1. Anderlini-D'Onofrio, Serena. The Lie with the Ounce of Truth: Lillian Hellman's Bisexual Fantasies

2. Armato, Philip M. "Good and Evil" in Lillian Hellman´s *The Children´s Hour*. Educational Theatre Journal Vol. 25, No. 4 (Dec., 1973), p.p. 443-447. Published by: The Johns Hopkins University Press

3. Barlow, E. Judith Plays by American Women 1930-1960. Applause. New York, London 1994

4. Bigsby, C.W. E. Modern American Drama 1945-2000. Cambridge University press, 2000

5. Bloom, Clive. American Drama. Macmillian, 1995

6. Brenshoff, Harry M. and Griffin, Sean. Queer images: a history of gay and lesbian film in America. — USA: Rowman & Littlefield Publishers, Inc., 2006

7. Friedman, Sharon. Feminism as Theme in Twentieth-Century American Women´s Drama. American Studies 25.1, 1984

8. Griffin, Alice and Thorsten, Geraldine. Understanding Lillian Hellman. University of South Carolina Press, 1999

9. Hellman, Lillian. Six plays by Lillian Hellman Vintage Books. A Division of Random House New York, 1979

10. Holmin, Ross. The Dramatic works of Lillian Hellman. Doctoral Dissertation Studia Anglestica Upsaliencia, 1973

11. Miller, Y. Jordan and Frazer, L. Winfred. American Drama between the Wars: A Critical History

12. Anderlini-D'Onofrio, Serena. The Lie with the Ounce of Truth: Lillian Hellman's Bisexual Fantasies

13. Titus, Mary. Murdering the Lesbian: Lillian Hellman's The Children's Hour Tulsa Studies in Women's Literature.Vol. 10, No. 2. Autumn, 1991

Internet Sources:

1.Article: Name in Lights….. Lillian Hellman. www.oldmagazinearticles.com Stage: march 15, 1939 page 46

2. IVCC Prof. Radek, Kimberly M. Women in the Twentieth Century and Beyond. http://www2.ivcc.edu/